MANIFESTING MIRACLES

SPECIFIC INSTRUCTIONS AND 36 ANSWERS TO YOUR QUESTIONS ABOUT MANIFESTATION

TAUGHT BY NEVILLE GODDARD

Part of the
NEVILLE EXPLAINS THE BIBLE
Series

CONTENTS

AT YOUR COMMAND

This book contains the very essence of the Principle of Expression. Had I cared to, I could have expanded it into a book of several hundred pages but such expansion would have defeated the purpose of this book.

Commands to be effective – must be short and to the point: the greatest command ever recorded is found in the few simple words, "And God said, 'Let there be light.'"

In keeping with this principle I now give to you, the reader, in these few pages, the truth as it was revealed to me.

-Neville-

AT YOUR COMMAND

Can man decree a thing and have it come to pass? Most decidedly he can! Man has always decreed that which has appeared in his world and is today decreeing that which is appearing in his world and shall continue to do so as long as man is conscious of being man. Not one thing has ever appeared in man's world but what man decreed that it should. This you may deny, but try as you will you cannot disprove it, for this decreeing is based upon a changeless principle. You do not command things to appear by your words or loud affirmations. Such vain repetition is more often than not confirmation of the opposite. Decreeing is ever done in consciousness. That is: every man is conscious of being that which he has decreed himself to be. The dumb man without using words is conscious of being dumb. Therefore he is decreeing himself to be dumb.

When the Bible is read in this light you will find it to be the greatest scientific book ever written. Instead of looking upon the Bible as the historical record of an ancient civilization or the biography of the unusual life of Jesus, see it as a great psychological drama taking place in the consciousness of man.

Claim it as your own and you will suddenly transform your world from the barren deserts of Egypt to the promised land of Canaan.

Everyone will agree with the statement that all things were made by God, and without him there is nothing made that is made, but what man does not agree upon is the identity of God. All the churches and priesthoods of the world disagree as to the identity and true nature of God. The Bible proves beyond the shadow of a doubt that Moses and the prophets were in one hundred per cent accord as to the identity and nature of God. And Jesus' life and teachings are in agreement with the findings of the prophets of old. Moses discovered God to be man's awareness of being, when he declared these little understood words, "I AM hath sent me unto you." David sang in his psalms, "Be still and know that I AM God." Isaiah declared, "I AM the Lord and there is none else. There is no God beside me. I girded thee, though thou hast not known me. I form the light, and create darkness; I make peace, and create evil. I the Lord do all these things."

The awareness of being as God is stated hundreds of times in the New Testament. To name but a few: "I AM the shepherd, I AM the door; I AM the resurrection and the life; I AM the way; I AM the Alpha and Omega; I AM the beginning and the end;" and again, "Whom do you say that I AM?"

It is not stated, "I, Jesus, am the door. I, Jesus am the way," nor is it said, "Whom do you say that I, Jesus, am?" It is clearly stated, "I AM the way." The awareness of being is the door through which the manifestations of life pass into the world of form.

Consciousness is the resurrecting power – resurrecting that which man is conscious of being. Man is ever out-picturing that which he is conscious of being. This is the truth that makes man free, for man is always self-imprisoned or self-freed.

If you, the reader, will give up all of your former beliefs in a God apart from yourself, and claim God as your awareness of being – as Jesus and the prophets did – you will transform your world with the realization that, "I and my father are one." This statement, "I and my father are one, but my father is greater than I," seems very confusing – but if interpreted in the light of what we have just said concerning the identity of God, you will find it very revealing. Consciousness, being God, is as 'father.' The thing that you are conscious of being is the 'son' bearing witness of his 'father.' It is like the conceiver and its conceptions. The conceiver is ever greater than his conceptions yet ever remains one with his conception. For instance: before you are conscious of being man, you are first conscious of being. Then you become conscious of being man. Yet you remain as conceiver, greater than your conception – man.

Jesus discovered this glorious truth and declared himself to be one with God – not a God that man had fashioned. For he never recognized such a God. He said, "If any man should ever come, saying, 'Look here or look there,' believe them not, for the kingdom of God is within you." Heaven is within you. Therefore, when it is recorded that "He went unto his father," it is telling you that he rose in consciousness to the point where he was just conscious of being, thus transcending the limitations of his present conception of himself, called 'Jesus.'

In the awareness of being all things are possible, he said, "You shall decree a thing and it shall come to pass." This is his decreeing – rising in consciousness to the naturalness of being the thing desired. As he expressed it, "And I, if I be lifted up, I shall draw all men unto me." If I be lifted up in consciousness to the naturalness of the thing desired I will draw the manifestation of that desire unto me. For he states, "No man comes unto me save the father within me draws him, and I and my father are one." Therefore, consciousness is the father that is drawing the manifestations of life unto you.

You are, at this very moment, drawing into your world that which you are now conscious of being. Now you can see what is meant by, "You must be born again." If you are dissatisfied with your present expression in life the only way to change it is to take your attention away from that which seems so real to you and rise in consciousness to that which you desire to be. You cannot serve two masters, therefore to take your attention from one state of consciousness and place it upon another is to die to one and live to the other.

The question, "Whom do you say that I AM?" is not addressed to a man called 'Peter' by one called 'Jesus.' This is the eternal question addressed to one's self by one's true being. In other words, "Whom do you say that you are?" For your conviction of yourself – your opinion of yourself – will determine your expression in life. He states, "You believe in God – believe also in me." In other words, it is the me within you that is this God.

Praying then, is seen to be recognizing yourself to be that which you now desire, rather than its accepting form of petitioning a God that does not exist for that which you now desire.

So can't you see why the millions of prayers are unanswered? Men pray to a God that does not exist. For instance: to be conscious of being poor and to pray to a God for riches is to be rewarded with that which you are conscious of being – which is poverty. Prayers to be successful must be claiming rather than begging – so if you would pray for riches turn from your picture of poverty by denying the very evidence of your senses and assume the nature of being wealthy.

We are told, "When you pray go within in secret and shut the door. And that which your father sees in secret, with that will he reward you openly." We have identified the 'father' to be the awareness of being. We have also identified the 'door' to be the awareness of being. So 'shutting the door' is shutting out that which 'I' am now aware of being and claiming myself to be that which 'I' desire to be. The very moment my claim is established to the point of conviction, that moment I begin to draw unto myself the evidence of my claim.

Do not question the how of these things appearing, for no man knows that way. That is, no manifestation knows how the things desired will appear.

Consciousness is the way or door through which things appear. He said, "I AM the way" – not 'I,' John Smith, am the way, but "I AM," the awareness of being, is the way through which the thing shall come. The signs always follow. They never precede. Things have no reality other than in consciousness. Therefore, get the consciousness first and the thing is compelled to appear.

You are told, "Seek ye first the kingdom of Heaven and all things shall be added unto you." Get first the consciousness of the things that you are seeking and leave the things alone. This is what is meant by "Ye shall decree a thing and it shall come to pass."

Apply this principle and you will know what it is to "prove me and see." The story of Mary is the story of every man. Mary was not a woman – giving birth in some miraculous way to one called 'Jesus.' Mary is the awareness of being that ever remains virgin, no matter how many desires it gives birth to. Right now look upon yourself as this virgin Mary – being impregnated by yourself through the medium of desire – becoming one with your desire to the point of embodying or giving birth to your desire.

For instance: it is said of Mary (whom you now know to be yourself) that she know not a man. Yet she conceived. That is, you, John Smith, have no reason to believe that that which you now desire is possible, but having discovered your awareness of being to be God, you make this awareness your husband and conceive a man child (manifestation) of the Lord, "For thy maker is thine husband; the Lord of hosts is his name; the Lord God of the whole earth shall he be called." Your ideal or ambition is this conception – the first command to her, which is now to yourself, is "Go, tell no man." That is, do not discuss your ambitions or desires with another for the other will only echo your present fears. Secrecy is the first law to be observed in realizing your desire.

The second, as we are told in the story of Mary, is to "Magnify the Lord." We have identified the Lord as your awareness of being. Therefore, to 'magnify the Lord' is to revalue or expand one's present conception of one's self to the point where this revaluation becomes natural. When this naturalness is attained you give birth by becoming that which you are one with in consciousness.

The story of creation is given us in digest form in the first chapter of John.

"In the beginning was the word." Now, this very second, is the 'beginning' spoken of. It is the beginning of an urge – a desire. 'The word' is the desire swimming around in your consciousness – seeking embodiment. The urge of itself has no reality, for, "I AM" or the awareness of being is the only reality. Things live only as long as I AM aware of being them; so to realize one's desire, the second line of this first verse of John must be applied. That is, "And the word was with God." The word, or desire, must be fixed or united with consciousness to give it reality. The awareness becomes aware of being the thing desired, thereby nailing itself upon the form or conception – and giving life unto its conception – or resurrecting that which was heretofore a dead or unfulfilled desire. "Two shall agree as touching anything and it shall be established on earth."

This agreement is never made between two persons. It is between the awareness and the thing desired. You are now conscious of being, so you are actually saying to yourself, without using words, "I AM." Now, if it is a state of health that you are desirous of attaining, before you have any evidence of health in your world, you begin to FEEL yourself to be healthy. And the very second the feeling "I AM healthy" is attained the two have agreed. That is, I AM and health have agreed to be one and this agreement ever results in the birth of a child which is the thing agreed upon – in this case, health. And because I made the agreement I express the thing agreed. So you can see why Moses stated, "I AM hath sent me." For what being, other than I AM could send you into expression? None – for "I AM the way – Beside me there is no other." If you take the wings of the morning and fly into the uttermost parts of the world or if you make your bed in Hell, you will still be aware of being. You are ever sent into expression by your awareness and your expression is ever that which you are aware of being.

Again, Moses stated, "I AM that I AM." Now here is something to always bear in mind. You cannot put new wine in old bottles or new patches upon old garments. That is: you cannot take with you into the new consciousness any part of the old man. All of your present beliefs, fears and limitations are weights that bind you to your present level of consciousness. If you would transcend this level you must leave behind all that is now your present self, or conception of yourself. To do this you take your attention away from all that is now your problem or limitation and dwell upon just being. That is: you say silently but feeling to yourself, "I AM." Do not condition this 'awareness' as yet. Just declare yourself to be, and continue to do so, until you are lost in the feeling of just being – faceless and formless. When this expansion of consciousness is attained, then, within this formless deep of yourself give form to the new conception by FEELING yourself to be THAT which you desire to be.

You will find within this deep of yourself all things to be divinely possible. Everything in the world which you can conceive of being, is to you, within this present formless awareness, a most natural attainment.

The invitation given us in the Scriptures is – "to be absent from the body and be present with the Lord." The 'body' being your former conception of yourself and 'the Lord' – your awareness of being. This is what is meant when Jesus said to Nicodemus, "Ye must be born again for except ye be born again ye cannot enter the kingdom of Heaven." That is: except you leave behind you your present conception of yourself and assume the nature of the new birth, you will continue to out-picture your present limitations.

The only way to change your expressions of life is to change your consciousness. For consciousness is the reality that eternally solidifies itself in the things round about you. Man's world in its every detail is his consciousness out-pictured. You can no more change your environment, or world, by destroying things than you can your reflection by destroying the mirror. Your environment, and all within it, reflects that which you are in consciousness. As long as you continue to be that in consciousness so long will you continue to out-picture it in your world.

Knowing this, begin to revalue yourself. Man has placed too little value upon himself. In the Book of Numbers you will read, "In that day there were giants in the land; and we were in our own sight as grasshoppers. And we were in their sight as grasshoppers." This does not mean a time in the dim past when man had the stature of giants. Today is the day – the eternal now – when conditions round about you have attained the appearance of giants (such as unemployed, the armies of your enemy, your problems and all things that seem to threaten you.) Those are the giant that make you feel yourself to be a grasshopper. But, you are told, you were first, in your own sight a grasshopper and because of this you were to the giants – a grasshopper. In other words, you can only be to others what you are first to yourself. Therefore, to revalue yourself and begin to feel yourself to be the giant, a center of power, is to dwarf these former giants and make of them grasshoppers. "All the inhabitants of the earth are as nothing, and he doeth according to his will in the armies of Heaven and among all the inhabitants of the earth; and none can stay his hand, nor say unto him, 'What doest thou?'" This being spoken of is not the orthodox God sitting in space but the one and only God – the everlasting father, your awareness of being. So awake to the power that you are, not as man, but as your true self, a faceless, formless awareness, and free yourself from your self-imposed prison.

"I am the good shepherd and know my sheep and am known of mine. My sheep hear my voice and I know them and they will follow me." Awareness is the good shepherd. What I am aware of being is the 'sheep' that follow me. So good a 'shepherd' is your awareness that it has never lost one of the 'sheep' that you are aware of being.

I am a voice calling in the wilderness of human confusion for such as I am aware of being, and never shall there come a time when that which I am convinced that I am shall fail to find me. "I AM" is an open door for all that I am to enter. Your awareness of being is lord and shepherd of your life. So, "The Lord is my shepherd; I shall not want" is seen in its true light now to be your consciousness. You could never be in want of proof or lack the evidence of that which you are aware of being.

This being true, why not become aware of being great; God-loving; wealthy; healthy; and all attributes that you admire?

It is just as easy to possess the consciousness of these qualities as it is to possess their opposites for you have not your present consciousness because of your world. On the contrary, your world is what it is because of your present consciousness. Simple, is it not? Too simple in fact for the wisdom of man that tries to complicate everything.

Paul said of this principle, "It is to the Greeks" (or wisdom of this world) "foolishness." "And to the Jews" (or those who look for signs) "a stumbling block"; with the result, that man continues to walk in darkness rather than awake to the being that he is. Man has so long worshipped the images of his own making that at first he finds this revelation blasphemous, since it spells death to all his previous beliefs in a God apart from himself. This revelation will bring the knowledge that "I and my father are one but my father is greater than I." You are one with your present conception of yourself. But you are greater than that which you are at present aware of being.

Before man can attempt to transform his world he must first lay the foundation – "I AM the Lord." That is, man's awareness, his consciousness of being is God. Until this is firmly established so that no suggestion or argument put forward by others can shake it, he will find himself returning to the slavery of his former beliefs. "If ye believe not that I AM he, ye shall die in your sins." That is, you shall continue to be confused and thwarted until you find the cause of your confusion. When you have lifted up the son of man then shall you know that I AM he, that is, that I, John Smith, do nothing of myself, but my father, or that state of consciousness which I am now one with does the works.

When this is realized every urge and desire that springs within you shall find expression in your world. "Behold I stand at the door and knock. If any man hear my voice and open the door I will come in to him and sup with him and he with me." The "I" knocking at the door is the urge.

The door is your consciousness. To open the door is to become one with that that which is knocking by FEELING oneself to be the thing desired. To feel one's desire as impossible is to shut the door or deny this urge expression. To rise in consciousness to the naturalness of the thing felt is to swing wide the door and invite this one into embodiment.

That is why it is constantly recorded that Jesus left the world of manifestation and ascended unto his father. Jesus, as you and I, found all things impossible to Jesus, as man. But having discovered his father to be the state of consciousness of the thing desired, he but left behind him the "Jesus consciousness" and rose in consciousness to that state desired and stood upon it until he became one with it. As he made himself one with that, he became that in expression.

This is Jesus' simple message to man: men are but garments that the impersonal being – I AM, the presence that men call God – dwells in. Each garment has certain limitations. In order to transcend these limitations and give expression to that which, as man – John Smith – you find yourself incapable of doing, you take your attention away from your present limitations, or John Smith conception of yourself, and merge yourself in the feeling of being that which you desire. Just how this desire or newly attained consciousness will embody itself, no man knows. For I, or the newly attained consciousness, has ways that ye know not of; its ways are past finding out. Do not speculate as to the HOW of this consciousness embodying itself, for no man is wise enough to know the how. Speculation is proof that you have not attained to the naturalness of being the thing desired and so are filled with doubts.

You are told, "He who lacks wisdom let him ask of God, that gives to all liberally, and upbraideth not; and it shall be given unto him. But let him ask not doubting for he who doubts is as a wave of the sea that is tossed and battered by the winds. And let not such a one think that he shall receive anything from the Lord." You can see why this statement is made, for only upon the rock of faith can anything be established. If you have not the consciousness of the thing you have not the cause or foundation upon which thing is erected.

A proof of this established consciousness is given you in the words, "Thank you, father." When you come into the joy of thanksgiving so that you actually feel grateful for having received that which is not yet apparent to the senses, you have definitely become one in consciousness with the thing for which you gave thanks. God (your awareness) is not mocked. You are ever receiving that which you are aware of being and no man gives thanks for something which he has not received. "Thank you father" is not, as it is used by many today, a sort of magical formula. You need never utter aloud the words, "Thank you, father." In applying this principle as you rise in consciousness to the point where you are really grateful and happy for having received the thing desired, you automatically rejoice and give thanks inwardly. You have already accepted the gift which was but a desire before you rose in consciousness, and your faith is now the substance that shall clothe your desire.

This rising in consciousness is the spiritual marriage where two shall agree upon being one and their likeness or image is established on earth.

"For whatsoever ye ask in my name the same give I unto you." 'Whatsoever' is quite a large measure. It is the unconditional. It does not state if society deems it right or wrong that you should ask it, it rests with you. Do you really want it? Do you desire it? That is all that is necessary. Life will give it to you if you ask 'in his name.'

His name is not a name that you pronounce with the lips. You can ask forever in the name of God or Jehovah or Christ Jesus and you will ask in vain. 'Name' means nature; so, when you ask in the nature of a thing, results ever follow. To ask in the name is to rise in consciousness and become one in nature with the thing desired, rise in consciousness to the nature of the thing, and you will become that thing in expression. Therefore, "what things soever ye desire, when ye pray, believe that ye receive them and ye shall receive them."

Praying, as we have shown you before, is recognition – the injunction to believe that ye receive is first person, present tense. This means that you must be in the nature of the things asked for before you can receive them.

To get into the nature easily, general amnesty is necessary. We are told, "Forgive if ye have aught against any, that your father also, which is in Heaven, may forgive you. But if ye forgive not, neither will your father forgive you." This may seem to be some personal God who is pleased or displeased with your actions but this is not the case.

Consciousness, being God, if you hold in consciousness anything against man, you are binding that condition in your world. But to release man from all condemnation is to free yourself so that you may rise to any level necessary; there is therefore, no condemnation to those in Christ Jesus.

Therefore, a very good practice before you enter into your meditation is first to free every man in the world from blame. For LAW is never violated and you can rest confidently in the knowledge that every man's conception of himself is going to be his reward. So you do not have to bother yourself about seeing whether or not man gets what you consider he should get. For life makes no mistakes and always gives man that which man first gives himself.

This brings us to that much abused statement of the Bible on tithing. Teachers of all kinds have enslaved man with this affair of tithing, for not themselves understanding the nature of tithing and being themselves fearful of lack, they have led their followers to believe that a tenth part of their income should be given to the Lord. Meaning, as they make very clear, that, when one gives a tenth part of his income to their particular organization he is giving his "tenth part" to the Lord – or is tithing. But remember, "I AM the Lord." Your awareness of being is the God that you give to and you ever give in this manner.

Therefore when you claim yourself to be anything, you have given that claim or quality to God. And your awareness of being, which is no respecter of persons, will return to you pressed down, shaken together, and running over with that quality or attribute which you claim for yourself.

Awareness of being is nothing that you could ever name. To claim God to be rich; to be great; to be love; to be all wise – is to define that which cannot be defined. For God is nothing that could ever be named.

Tithing is necessary and you do tithe with God. But from now on give to the only God and see to it that you give him the quality that you desire as man to express by claiming yourself to be the great, the wealthy, the loving, the all wise.

Do not speculate as to how you shall express these qualities or claims, for life has a way that you, as man, know not of. Its ways are past finding out. But, I assure you, the day you claim these qualities to the point of conviction, your claims will be honored. There is nothing covered that shall not be uncovered. That which is spoken in secret shall be proclaimed from the housetops. That is, your secret convictions of yourself – these secret claims that no man knows of, when really believed, will be shouted from the housetops in your world. For your convictions of yourself are the words of the God within you, which words are spirit and cannot return unto you void but must accomplish whereunto they are sent.

You are at this moment calling out of the infinite that which you are now conscious of being. And not one word or conviction will fail to find you.

"I AM the vine and ye are the branches." Consciousness is the 'vine,' and those qualities which you are now conscious of being are as 'branches' that you feed and keep alive. Just as a branch has no life except it be rooted in the vine, so likewise things have no life except you be conscious of them. Just as a branch withers and dies if the sap of the vine ceases to flow towards it, so do things in your world pass away if you take your attention from them, because your attention is as the sap of life that keeps alive and sustains the things of your world.

To dissolve a problem that now seems so real to you all that you do is remove your attention from it. In spite of its seeming reality, turn from it in consciousness. Become indifferent and begin to feel yourself to be that which would be the solution of the problem.

For instance: if you were imprisoned no man would have to tell you that you should desire freedom. Freedom, or rather the desire of freedom would be automatic. So why look behind the four walls of your prison bars? Take your attention from being imprisoned and begin to feel yourself to be free. FEEL it to the point where it is natural – the very second you do so, those prison bars will dissolve. Apply this same principle to any problem.

I have seen people who were in debt up to their ears apply this principle and in the twinkling of an eye debts that were mountainous were removed. I have seen those whom doctors had given up as incurable take their attention away from their problem of disease and begin to feel themselves to be well in spite of the evidence of their sense to the contrary. In no time at all this so called "incurable disease" vanished and left no scar.

Your answer to, "Whom do you say that I AM?" ever determines your expression. As long as you are conscious of being imprisoned or diseased, or poor, so long will you continue to out-picture or express these conditions.

When man realized that he is now that which he is seeking and begins to claim that he is, he will have the proof of his claim. This cue is given you in words, "Whom seek ye?" And they answered, "Jesus." And the voice said, "I am he." 'Jesus' here means salvation or savior. You are seeking to be salvaged from that which is not your problem.

"I am" is he that will save you. If you are hungry, your savior is food. If you are poor, your savior is riches. If you are imprisoned, your savior is freedom. If you are diseased, it will not be a man called Jesus who will save you, but health will become your savior. Therefore, claim "I am he," in other words, claim yourself to be the thing desired. Claim it in consciousness – not in words – and consciousness will reward you with your claim. You are told, "You shall find me when you FEEL after me." Well, FEEL after that quality in consciousness until you FEEL yourself to be it. When you lose yourself in the feeling of being it, the quality will embody itself in your world.

You are healed from your problem when you touch the solution of it. "Who has touched me? For I perceive virtue is gone out of me." Yes, the day you touch this being within you – FEELING yourself to be cured or healed, virtues will come out of your very self and solidify themselves in your world as healings.

It is said, "You believe in God. Believe also in me for I am he." Have the faith of God. "He made himself one with God and found it not robbery to do the works of God." Go you and do likewise.

Yes, begin to believe your awareness, your consciousness of being to be God. Claim for yourself all the attributes that you have heretofore given an external God and you will begin to express these claims.

"For I am not a God afar off. I am nearer than your hands and feet – nearer than your very breathing." I am your awareness of being. I am that in which all that I shall ever be aware of being shall begin and end. "For before the world was I AM; and when the world shall cease to be, I AM; before Abraham was, I AM." This I AM is your awareness.

"Except the Lord build the house they labor in vain that build it." 'The Lord,' being your consciousness, except that which you seek is first established in your consciousness, you will labor in vain to find it. All things must begin and end in consciousness.

So, blessed indeed is the man that trusteth in himself – for man's faith in God will ever be measured by his confidence in himself. You believe in a God, believe also in ME.

Put not your trust in men for men but reflect the being that you are, and can only bring to you or do unto you that which you have first done unto yourself.

"No man taketh away my life, I lay it down myself." I have the power to lay it down and the power to take it up again.

No matter what happens to man in this world it is never an accident. It occurs under the guidance of an exact and changeless Law.

"No man" (manifestation) "comes unto me except the father within me draw him," and "I and my father are one." Believe this truth and you will be free. Man has always blamed others for that which he is and will continue to do so until he find himself as cause of all. "I AM" comes not to destroy but to fulfill. "I AM," the awareness within you, destroys nothing but ever fill full the molds or conception one has of one's self.

It is impossible for the poor man to find wealth in this world no matter how he is surrounded with it until he first claims himself to be wealthy. For signs follow, they do not precede. To constantly kick and complain against the limitations of poverty while remaining poor in consciousness is to play the fool's game. Changes cannot take place from that level of consciousness for life is constantly out-picturing all levels.

Follow the example of the prodigal son. Realize that you, yourself brought about this condition of waste and lack and make the decision within yourself to rise to a higher level where the fatted calf, the ring, and the robe await your claim.

There was no condemnation of the prodigal when he had the courage to claim this inheritance as his own. Others will condemn us only as long as we continue in that for which we condemn ourselves. So: "Happy is the man that condemneth himself not in that which he alloweth." For to life nothing is condemned. All is expressed.

Life does not care whether you call yourself rich or poor; strong or weak. It will eternally reward you with that which you claim as true of yourself.

The measurements of right and wrong belong to man alone. To life there is nothing right or wrong. As Paul stated in his letters to the Romans: "I know and am persuaded by the Lord Jesus that there is nothing unclean of itself, but to him that esteemeth anything to be unclean, to him it is unclean." Stop asking yourself whether you are worthy or unworthy to receive that which you desire. You, as man, did not create the desire. Your desires are ever fashioned within you because of what you now claim yourself to be.

When a man is hungry, (without thinking) he automatically desires food. When imprisoned, he automatically desires freedom and so forth. Your desires contain within themselves the plan of self-expression.

So leave all judgments out of the picture and rise in consciousness to the level of your desire and make yourself one with it by claiming it to be so now. For: "My grace is sufficient for thee. My strength is made perfect in weakness."

Have faith in this unseen claim until the conviction is born within you that it is so. Your confidence in this claim will pay great rewards. Just a little while and he, the thing desired, will come. But without faith it is impossible to realize anything. Through faith the worlds were framed because "faith is the substance of the thing hoped for – the evidence of the thing not yet seen."

Don't be anxious or concerned as to results. They will follow just as surely as day follows night.

Look upon your desires – all of them – as the spoken words of God, and every word or desire a promise. The reason most of us fail to realize our desires is because we are constantly conditioning them. Do not condition your desire. Just accept it as it comes to you. Give thanks for it to the point that you are grateful for having already received it – then go about your way in peace.

Such acceptance of your desire is like dropping seed – fertile seed – into prepared soil. For when you can drop the thing desired in consciousness, confident that it shall appear, you have done all that is expected to you. But, to be worried or concerned about the HOW of your desire maturing is to hold these fertile seeds in a mental grasp, and, therefore, never to have dropped them in the soil of confidence.

The reason men condition their desires is because they constantly judge after the appearance of being and see the things as real – forgetting that the only reality is the consciousness back of them.

To see things as real is to deny that all things are possible to God. The man who is imprisoned and sees his four walls as real is automatically denying the urge or promise of God within him of freedom.

A question often asked when this statement is made is: if one's desire is a gift of God how can you say that if one desires to kill a man that such a desire is good and therefore God sent? In answer to this let me say that no man desires to kill another. What he does desire is to be freed from such a one. But because he does not believe that the desire to be free from such a one contains within itself the powers of freedom, he conditions that desire and sees the only way to express such freedom is to destroy the man – forgetting that the life wrapped within the desire has ways that he, as man, knows not of. Its ways are past finding out. Thus man distorts the gifts of God through his lack of faith.

Problems are the mountains spoken of that can be removed if one has but the faith of a grain of a mustard seed. Men approach their problem as did the old lady who, on attending service and hearing the priest say, "If you had but the faith of a grain of a mustard seed you would say unto yonder mountain 'be thou removed' and it shall be removed and nothing is impossible to you."

That night as she said her prayers, she quoted this part of the scriptures and retired to bed in what she thought was faith. On arising in the morning she rushed to the window and exclaimed: "I knew that old mountain would still be there."

For this is how man approaches his problem. He knows that they are still going to confront him. And because life is no respecter of persons and destroys nothing, it continues to keep alive that which he is conscious of being.

Things will disappear only as man changes in consciousness. Deny it if you will, it still remains a fact that consciousness is the only reality and things but mirror that which you are in consciousness. So the heavenly state you are seeking will be found only in consciousness, for the kingdom of heaven is within you. As the will of heaven is ever done on earth you are today living in the heaven that you have established within you. For here on this very earth your heaven reveals itself. The kingdom of heaven really is at hand. NOW is the accepted time. So create a new heaven, enter into a new state of consciousness and a new earth will appear.

"The former things shall pass away. They shall not be remembered not come into mind any more. For behold, I," (your consciousness) "come quickly and my reward is with me."

I am nameless but will take upon myself every name (nature) that you call me. Remember it is you, yourself, that I speak of as 'me.' So every conception that you have of yourself – that is every deep conviction – you have of yourself is that which you shall appear as being – for I AM not fooled; God is not mocked.

Now let me instruct you in the art of fishing. It is recorded that the disciples fished all night and caught nothing. Then Jesus came upon the scene and told them to cast their nets in once more, into the same waters that only a moment before were barren – and this time their nets were bursting with the catch.

This story is taking place in the world today right within you, the reader. For you have within you all the elements necessary to go fishing. But until you find that Jesus Christ, (your awareness) is Lord, you will fish, as did these disciples, in the night of human darkness. That is, you will fish for THINGS thinking things to be real and will fish with the human bait – which is a struggle and an effort – trying to make contact with this one and that one: trying to coerce this being or the other being; and all such effort will be in vain. But when you discover your awareness of being to be Christ Jesus you will let him direct your fishing. And you will fish in consciousness for the things that you desire. For your desire – will be the fish that you will catch, because your consciousness is the only living reality you will fish in the deep waters of consciousness.

If you would catch that which is beyond your present capacity you must launch out into deeper waters, for, within your present consciousness such fish or desires cannot swim. To launch out into deeper waters, you leave behind you all that is now your present problem, or limitation, by taking your ATTENTION AWAY from it. Turn your back completely upon every problem and limitation that you now possess.

Dwell upon just being by saying, "I AM," "I AM," "I AM," to yourself. Continue to declare to yourself that you just are. Do not condition this declaration, just continue to FEEL yourself to be and without warning you will find yourself slipping the anchor that tied you to the shallow of your problems and moving out into the deep.

This is usually accompanied with the feeling of expansion. You will FEEL yourself expand as though you were actually growing. Don't be afraid, for courage is necessary. You are not going to die to anything by your former limitations, but they are going to die as you move away from them, for they live only in your consciousness. In this deep or expanded consciousness you will find yourself to be a power that you had never dreamt of before.

The things desired before you shoved off from the shores of limitation are the fish you are going to catch in this deep. Because you have lost all consciousness of your problems and barriers, it is now the easiest thing in the world to FEEL yourself to be one with the things desired.

Because I AM (your consciousness) is the resurrection and the life, you must attach this resurrecting power that you are to the thing desired if you would make it appear and live in your world. Now you begin to assume the nature of the thing desired by feeling, "I AM wealthy"; "I AM free"; "I AM strong." When these 'FEELS' are fixed within yourself, your formless being will take upon itself the forms of the things felt. You become 'crucified' upon the feelings of wealth, freedom, and strength. Remain buried in the stillness of these convictions. Then, as a thief in the night and when you least expect it, these qualities will be resurrected in your world as living realities.

The world shall touch you and see that you are flesh and blood for you shall begin to bear fruit of the nature of these qualities newly appropriated.

This is the art of successful fishing for the manifestations of life.

Successful realization of the thing desired is also told us in the story of Daniel in the lion's den. Here, it is recorded that Daniel, while in the lion's den, turned his back upon the lions and looked towards the light coming from above; that the lions remained powerless and Daniel's faith in his God saved him.

This also is your story and you too must do as Daniel did. If you found yourself in a lion's den you would have no other concern but lions. You would not be thinking of one thing in the world but your problem – which problem would be lions.

Yet, you are told that Daniel turned his back upon them and looked towards the light that was his God. If we would follow the example of Daniel we would, while imprisoned within the den of poverty of sickness, take our attention away from our problems of debts or sickness and dwell upon the thing we seek.

If we do not look back in consciousness to our problems but continue in faith – believing ourselves to be that which we seek, we too will find our prison walls open and the thing sought – yes, "whatsoever things" – realized.

Another story is told us: of the widow and the three drops of oil. The prophet asked the widow, "What have ye in your house?" And she replied, "Three drops of oil." He then said to her, "Go borrow vessels. Close the door after ye have returned into your house and begin to pour." And she poured from three drops of oil into all the borrowed vessels, filling them to capacity with oil remaining.

You, the reader, are this widow. You have not a husband to impregnate you or make you fruitful, for a 'widow' is a barren state. Your awareness is now the Lord – or the prophet that has become your husband.

Follow the example of the widow, who instead of recognizing an emptiness or nothingness, recognized the something – three drops of oil.

Then the command to her, "Go within and close the door," that is, shut the door of the senses that tell you of the empty measures, the debts, the problems.

When you have taken your attention away completely by shutting out the evidence of the senses, begin to FEEL the joy (symbolized by oil) of having received the things desired. When the agreement is established within you so that all doubts and fears have passed away, then, you too will fill all the empty measures of your life and will have an abundance running over.

Recognition is the power that conjures in the world. Every state that you have ever recognized, you have embodied. That which you are recognizing as true of yourself today is that which you are experiencing. So be as the widow and recognize joy, no matter how little the beginnings of recognition, and you will be generously rewarded – for the world is a magnified mirror, magnifying everything that you are conscious of being.

"I AM the Lord the God, which has brought thee out of the land of Egypt, out of the house of bondage; thou shalt have no other gods before me." What a glorious revelation, your awareness now revealed as the Lord thy God! Come, awake from your dream of being imprisoned. Realize that the earth is yours, "and the fullness thereof; the world, and all that dwells therein."

You have become so enmeshed in the belief that you are man that you have forgotten the glorious being that you are. Now with your memory restored DECREE the unseen to appear and it SHALL appear, for all things are compelled to respond to the Voice of God, Your awareness of being – the world is AT YOUR COMMAND!

36 QUESTIONS
AND ANSWERS

1

What is the meaning of the insignia on your book covers?

It is an eye imposed upon a heart which, in turn, is imposed upon a tree laden with fruit; meaning that what you are conscious of, and accept as true, you are going to realize. As a man thinketh in his heart, so he is.

2

I would like to be married, but have not found the right man. How do I imagine a husband?

Forever in love with ideals, it is the ideal state that captures the mind. Do not confine the state of marriage to a certain man, but a full, rich and overflowing life. You desire to experience the joy of marriage. Do not modify your dream, but enhance it by making it lovelier. Then condense your desire into a single sensation, or act, which implies its fulfillment.

In this western world a woman wears a wedding ring on the third finger of her left hand. Motherhood need not imply marriage; intimacy need not imply marriage, but a wedding ring does.

Relax in a comfortable arm chair, or lie flat on your back and induce a state akin to sleep. Then assume the feeling of being married. Imagine a wedding band on your finger. Touch it. Turn it around the finger. Pull it off over the knuckle. Keep the action going until the ring has the distinctness and feeling of reality. Become so lost in feeling the ring on your finger that when you open your eyes, you will be surprised that it is not there.

If you are a man who does not wear a ring, you could assume greater responsibility. How would you feel if you had a wife to care for? Assume the feeling of being a happily married man right now.

3

What must I do to inspire creative thoughts such as those needed for writing?

What must you do? Assume the story has already been written and accepted by a great publishing house. Reduce the idea of being a writer to the sensation of satisfaction.

Repeat the phrase, "Isn't it wonderful!" or "Thank you, thank you, thank you," over and over again until you feel successful. Or, imagine a friend congratulating you. There are unnumbered ways of implying success, but always go to the end. Your acceptance of the end wills its fulfillment.

Do not think about getting in the mood to write, but live and act as though you are now the author you desire to be. Assume you have the talent for writing. Think of the pattern you want displayed on the outside. If you write a book and no one is willing to buy it, there is no satisfaction. Act as though people are hungry for your work. Live as though you cannot produce stories or books fast enough to meet the demand. Persist in this assumption and all that is necessary to achieve your goal will quickly burst into bloom and you will express it.

4

How do I imagine larger audiences for my talks?

I can answer you best by sharing the technique used by a very able teacher I know. When this man first came to this country he began speaking in a small hall in New York City. Although only fifty or sixty people attended his Sunday morning meeting, and they sat in front, this teacher would stand at the podium and imagine a vast audience. Then he would say to the empty space, "Can you hear me back there?"

Today this man is speaking in Carnegie Hall in New York City to approximately 2,500 people every Sunday morning and Wednesday evening. He wanted to speak to crowds. He was not modest. He did not try to fool himself but built a crowd in his own consciousness, and crowds come. Stand before a large audience. Address this audience in your imagination. Feel you are on that stage and your feeling will provide the means.

5

Is it possible to imagine several things at the same time, or should I confine my imagining to one desire?

Personally I like to confine my imaginal act to a single thought, but that does not mean I will stop there. During the course of a day I may imagine many things, but instead of imagining lots of small things, I would suggest that you imagine something so big it includes all the little things. Instead of imagining wealth, health and friends, imagine being ecstatic. You could not be ecstatic and be in pain. You could not be ecstatic and be threatened with a dispossession notice. You could not be ecstatic if you were not enjoying a full measure of friendship and love.

What would the feeling be like were you ecstatic without knowing what had happened to produce your ecstasy? Reduce the idea of ecstasy to the single sensation, "Isn't it wonderful!" Do not allow the conscious, reasoning mind to ask why, because if it does it will start to look for visible causes, and then the sensation will be lost. Rather, repeat over and over again, "Isn't it wonderful!" Suspend judgment as to what is wonderful. Catch the one sensation of the wonder of it all and things will happen to bear witness to the truth of this sensation. And I promise you, it will include all the little things.

6

How often should I perform the imaginal act, a few days or several weeks?

In the Book of Genesis the story is told of Jacob wrestling with an angel. This story gives us the clue we are looking for: that when satisfaction is reached, impotence follows.

When the feeling of reality is yours, for the moment at least, you are mentally impotent. The desire to repeat the act of prayer is lost, having been replaced by the feeling of accomplishment. You cannot persist in wanting what you already have. If you assume you are what you desire to be to the point of ecstasy, you no longer want it. Your imaginal act is as much a creative act as a physical one – wherein man halts, shrinks and is blessed. For as man creates his own likeness, so does your imaginal act transform itself into the likeness of your assumption. If, however, you do not reach the point of satisfaction, repeat the action over and over again until you feel as though you touched it and virtue went out of you.

7

I have been taught not to ask for earthly things, only for spiritual growth, yet money and things are what I need.

You must be honest with yourself. All through scripture the question is asked, "What do you want of me?"

Some wanted to see, others to eat, and still others wanted to be made straight, or "That my child live."

Your dimensionally larger self speaks to you through the language of desire. Do not deceive yourself. Knowing what you want, claim already have it, for it is your Father's good pleasure to give it to you and remember, what you desire, that you have.

8

When you have assumed your desire, do you keep in mind the ever-presence of this Greater One protecting and giving you your assumption?

The acceptance of the end wills the means. Assume the feeling of your wish fulfilled and your dimensionally greater self will determine the means. When you appropriate a state as though you had it, the activity of the day will divert your mind from all anxious thoughts so that you do not look for signs. You do not have to carry the feeling that some presence is going to do it for you, rather you know it is already done. Knowing it is already a fact, walk as though it were, and things will happen to make it so. You do not have to be concerned about some presence doing anything for you. The deeper, dimensionally greater you has already done it. All you do is move to the place where you encounter it.

Remember the story of the man who left the master and was on his way home when he met his servant who said, "Your son lives." And when he asked at what hour it was done the servant replied, "The seventh hour." The self-same hour that he assumed his desire, it was done for him, for it was at the seventh hour that the master said, "Your son lives."

Your desire is already granted. Walk as though it were and, although time beats slowly in this dimension of your being, it will nevertheless bring you confirmation of your assumption. I ask you not to be impatient, though. If there is one thing you really have need of, it is patience.

9

Isn't there a law that says you cannot get something for nothing? Must we not earn what we desire?

Creation is finished! It is your Father's good pleasure to give you the kingdom. The parable of the prodigal son is your answer. In spite of man's waste, when he comes to his senses and remembers who he is, he feeds on the fatted calf of abundance and wears the robe and ring of authority.

There is nothing to earn. Creation was finished in the foundation of time. You, as man, are God made visible for the purpose of displaying what is, not what is to be. Do not think you must work out your salvation by the sweat of your brow. It is not four months until the harvest, the fields are already white, simply thrust in the sickle.

10

Does not the thought that creation is finished rob one of his initiative?

If you observe an event before it occurs, then the occurring event must be predetermined from the point of view of being awake in this three-dimensional world. Yet, you do not have to encounter what you observe. You can, by changing your concept of self, interfere with your future and mold it in harmony with your changed concept of self.

11

Does not this ability to change the future deny that creation is finished?

No. You, by changing your concept of self, change your relationship to things. If you rearrange the words of a play to write a different one, you have not created new words, but simply had the joy of rearranging them. Your concept of self determines the order of events you encounter. They are in the foundation of the world, but not their order of arrangement.

12

Why should one who works hard in metaphysics always seem to lack?

Because he has not really applied metaphysics. I am not speaking of a mamby-pamby approach to life, but a daily application of the law of consciousness. When you appropriate your good, there is no need for a man, or state, to act as a medium through which your good will come.

Living in a world of men, money is needed in my everyday life. If I invite you to lunch tomorrow, I must pick up the check. When I leave the hotel, I must pay the bill. In order to take the train back to New York my railway fare must be paid. I need money and it has to be there. I am not going to say, "God knows best, and He knows I need money." Rather, I will appropriate the money as though it were!

We must live boldly! We must go through life as though we possessed what we want to possess. Do not think that because you helped another, someone outside of you saw your good works and will give you something to ease your burden. There is no one to do it for you. You, yourself, must go boldly on appropriating what your Father has already given you.

13

Can an uneducated person educate himself by assuming the feeling of being educated?

Yes. An aroused interest is awarded information from every side. You must sincerely desire to be well schooled. The desire to be well read, followed by the assumption that you are, makes you selective in your reading. As you progress in your education, you automatically become more selective, more discriminating in all that you do.

14

My husband and I are taking the class together. Should we discuss our desires with each other?

There are two spiritual sayings which permeate the Bible. One is, "Go tell no man," and the other is "I have told you before it comes to pass that when it does come to pass you may believe."

It takes spiritual boldness to tell another that your desire is fulfilled before it is seen on the outside. If you do not have that kind of boldness, then you had better keep quiet.

I personally enjoy telling my plans to my wife, because we both get such a thrill when they come into being. The first person a man wants to prove this law to is his wife. It is said that Mohammad is everlastingly great because his first disciple was his wife.

15

Should my husband and I work on the same project or on separate ones?

That is entirely up to you. My wife and I have different interests, yet we have much in common. Do you recall the story I told of our return to the United States this spring? I felt it was my duty as a husband to get passage back to America, so I appropriated that to myself. I feel there are certain things that are on my wife's side of the contract, such as maintaining a clean, lovely home and finding the appropriate school for our daughter, so she takes care of those.

Quite often my wife will ask me to imagine for her, as though she has greater faith in my ability to do it than in her own. That flatters me because every man worthy of the name wants to feel that his family has faith in him. But I see nothing wrong in the communion between two who love one another.

16

I would think that if you get too much into the sleepy state there would be a lack of feeling.

When I speak of feeling I do not mean emotion, but acceptance of the fact that the desire is fulfilled.

Feeling grateful, fulfilled, or thankful, it is easy to say, "Thank You," "Isn't it wonderful!" or "It is finished."

When you get into the state of thankfulness, you can either awaken knowing it is done, or fall asleep in the feeling of the wish fulfilled.

17

Is love a product of your own consciousness?

All things exist in your consciousness, be they love or hate. Nothing comes from without. The hills to which you look for help are those of an inner range.

Your feelings of love, hate or indifference all spring from your own consciousness. You are infinitely greater than you could ever conceive yourself to be. Never in eternity will you reach the ultimate you. That is how wonderful you are. Love is not a product of you – you are love. For that is what God is, and God's name is "I Am" – the very name you call yourself before you make the claim as to the state you are now in.

18

Suppose my wants cannot materialize for six months to a year, do I wait to imagine them?

When the desire is upon you, that is the time to accept your wish in its fullness. Perhaps there are reasons why the urge is given to you at this time. Your three-dimensional being may think it cannot be now, but your fourth dimensional mind knows it already is, so the desire should be accepted by you as a physical fact now.

Suppose you wanted to build a house. The urge to have it is now, but it is going to take time for the trees to grow and the carpenter to build the house. Although the urge seems big, do not wait to adjust to it. Claim possession now and let it objectify itself in its own strange way. Do not say it will take six months or a year. The minute the desire comes upon you, assume it is already a fact!

You and you alone have given your desire a time interval and time is relative when it comes to this world. Do not wait for anything to come to pass, accept it now as though it were and see what happens.

When you have a desire, the deeper you, who men call God, is speaking. He urges you, through the language of desire, to accept that which is not that which is to be! Desire is simply His communion with you, telling you that your desire is yours, now! Your acceptance of this fact is proved by your complete adjustment to it as though it were true.

19

Why do some of us die young?

Our lives are not – in retrospect – measured by years, but by the content of those years.

20

What would you consider a full life?

A variety of experiences. The more varied they are, the richer is your life. At death you function in a dimensionally larger world, and play your part on a keyboard made up of a lifetime of human experiences. Therefore, the more varied your experiences, the finer is your instrument, and the richer is your life.

21

What about a child who dies at birth?

The child who is born, lives forever, as nothing dies. It may appear that the child who dies at birth has no keyboard of human experience, but as a poet once said:

"He drew a circle that shut me out – Infidel, scoundrel, a thing to flout. But Love and I had the wit to win: We drew a circle that took him in!"

The loved one has access to the sensory experiences of the lover. God is love; therefore, ultimately everyone has an instrument, the keyboard of which is the sensory impressions of all men.

22

What is your technique of prayer?

It starts with desire, for desire is the mainspring of action. You must know and define your objective, then condense it into a sensation which implies fulfillment.

When your desire is clearly defined, immobilize your physical body and experience – in your imagination – the action which implies its fulfillment. Repeat this act over and over again until it has the vividness and feeling of reality.

Or condense your desire into a single phrase that implies fulfillment – such as, "Thank you Father," "Isn't it wonderful," or "It is finished."

Repeat that condensed phrase, or action in your imagination, over and over again. Then either awaken from that state, or slip off into the deep. It does not matter, for the act is done when you completely accept it as being finished in that sleepy, drowsy state.

23

Two people want the same position. One has it. The other had it and now wants it back.

Your Father (the dimensionally greater you) has ways and means you know not of. Accept His wisdom. Feel your desire is fulfilled, then allow your Father to give it to you. The present one may be promoted to a higher position, or marry a man of great wealth and give up her job. She may come into a great deal of money, or choose to move to another state.

Many people say they want to work, but I question that seriously. They want security and condition security on a job. But I really do not think the average girl truly wants to get up in the morning and go to work.

24

What is the cause of disease and pain?

The physical body is an emotional filter. Many human ailments, hitherto considered purely physical, are now recognized as rooted in emotional disturbances.

Pain comes from lack of relaxation. When you sleep there is no pain. If you are under an anesthetic, there is no pain because you are relaxed, as it were. If you have pain it is because you are tense and trying to force something.

You cannot force an idea into embodiment, you simply appropriate it. It is attention minus effort. Only practice will bring you to that point where you can be attentive and still be relaxed.

Attention is tension toward an end, and relaxation is just the opposite. Here are two completely opposite ideas that you must blend until you learn, through practice, how to be attentive, but not tense. The word "contention" means "attention minus effort." In the state of contention you are held by the idea without tension.

25

No matter how much I try to be happy, underneath, I have a melancholy feeling of being left out. Why?

Because you feel you are not wanted.

Were I you, I would assume I am wanted. You know the technique. The assumption that you are wanted may seem false when first assumed, but if you will feel wanted and respected, and persist in that assumption, you will be amazed how others will seek you out. They will begin to see qualities in you they had never seen before. I promise you. If you will but assume you are wanted, you will be.

26

If security came to me through the death of a loved one, did I bring about that death?

Do not think for one second that you brought about a death by assuming security. The greater you is not going to injure anyone. It sees all and, knowing the length of life of all, it can inspire the other to give you that which can fulfill your assumption.

You did not kill the person who named you in his will. If, a few days after your complete acceptance of the idea of security, Uncle John made his exit from this three-dimensional plane and left you his estate, it is only because it was time for Uncle John to go. He did not die one second before his time, however. The greater you saw the life span of John and used him as the way to bring about the fulfillment of your feeling of security.

The acceptance of the end wills the means toward the fulfillment of that end. Do not be concerned with anything save the end. Always bear in mind that the responsibility to make it so is completely removed from your shoulders. It is yours because you accept it as so!

27

I have more than one objective. Would it be ineffective to concentrate on different objectives at different periods of concentration?

I like to take one consuming ambition, restrict it to a single short phrase, or act that implies fulfillment, but I do not limit my ambition. I only know that my real objective will include all the little ones.

28

I find it difficult to change my concept of self. Why?

Because your desire to change has not been aroused. If you would fall in love with what you really want to be, you would become it. It takes an intense hunger to bring about a transformation of self.

"As the hart panteth after the water brooks, so panteth my soul after thee, O Lord." If you would become as thirsty for perfection as the little hart is for water that it braves the anger of the tiger in the forest, you would become perfect.

29

I am contemplating a business venture. It means a great deal to me, but I cannot imagine how it can come into being.

You are relieved of that responsibility. You do not have to make it a reality, it already is!

Although your concept of self seems so far removed from the venture you now contemplate, it exists now as a reality within you. Ask yourself how you would feel and what you would be doing if your business venture were a great success. Become identified with that character and feeling and you will be amazed how quickly you will realize your dream.

The only sacrifice you are called upon to make is to give up your present concept of self and appropriate the desire you want to express.

30

As a metaphysical student I have been taught to believe that race beliefs and universal assumptions affect me. Do you mean that only to the degree I give these universal beliefs power over me, am I influenced by them?

Yes. It is only your individual viewpoint, as your world is forever bearing witness to your present concept of self. If someone offends you, change your concept of self. That is the only way others change.

Tonight's paper may be read by any six people in this room and no two will interpret the same story in the same way. One will be elated, the other depressed, another indifferent, and so on, yet it is the same story.

Universal assumptions, race beliefs, call them what you will, they are not important to you. What is important is your concept, not of another, but of yourself. For the concept you hold of yourself determines the concept you hold of others. Leave others alone. What are they to you? Follow your own desires.

The law is always in operation, always absolute. Your consciousness is the rock upon which all structures rest. Watch what you are aware of. You need not concern yourself with others because you are sustained by the absoluteness of this law. No man comes to you of his own accord, be he good, bad or indifferent. He did not choose you! You chose him! He was drawn to you because of what you are.

You cannot destroy the state another represents through force. Rather, leave him alone. What is he to you? Rise to a higher level of consciousness and you will find a new world awaiting you, and as you sanctify yourself, others are sanctified.

31

Who wrote the Bible?

The Bible was written by intelligent men who used solar and phallic myths to reveal psychological truths. But we have mistaken their allegory for history and, therefore, have failed to see their true message.

It is strange, but when the Bible was launched upon the world, and acceptance seemed to be in sight, the great Alexandria Library was burnt to the ground, leaving no record as to how the Bible came into being. Few people can read other languages, so they cannot compare their beliefs with others. Our churches do not encourage us to compare. How many of the millions who accept the Bible as fact, ever question it? Believing it is the word of God, they blindly accept the words and thus lose the essence they contain. Having accepted the vehicle, they do not understand what the vehicle conveys.

32

Do you use the Apocrypha?

Not in my teaching. I have several volumes of them at home. They are no greater than the sixty-six books of our present Bible. They are simply telling the same truth in a different way. For instance, the story is told of Jesus, as a young boy, watching children make birds out of mud. Holding the birds in their hands, they pretend the birds are flying. Jesus approaches and knocks the birds out of their hands. As they begin to cry, he picks up one of the broken birds and re-molds it. Holding it high, he breaths upon it and the bird takes wing.

Here is a story of one who came to break the idols in the minds of men, then show them how to use the same substance and re-mold it into a beautiful form and give it life. That is what this story is trying to convey. "I come, not to bring peace, but a sword." Truth slays all the little mud hens of the mind, slays illusions and then re-molds them into a new pattern which sets man free.

33

If Jesus was a fictional character created by Biblical writers for the purpose of illustrating certain psychological dramas, how do you account for the fact that he and his philosophy are mentioned in the nonreligious and non-Christian history of those times? Were not Pontius Pilate and Herod real flesh and blood Roman officials in those days?

The story of Jesus is the identical story as that of the Hindu savior, Krishna. They are the same psychological characters. Both were supposed to have been born of virgin mothers. The rulers of the time sought to destroy them when they were children. Both healed the sick, resurrected the dead, taught the gospel of love and died a martyr's death for mankind. Hindus and Christians alike believe their savior to be God made man.

Today people quote Socrates, yet the only proof that Socrates ever existed is in the works of Plato. It is said that Socrates drank hemlock – but I ask you, who is Socrates?

I once quoted a line from Shakespeare and a lady said to me, "But Hamlet said that." Hamlet never said it – Shakespeare wrote the lines and put the words in the mouth of a character he created and named Hamlet.

St. Augustine once said, "That which is now called the Christian religion existed among the ancients. They began to call Christianity the true religion, yet it never existed."

34

Do you use affirmations and denials?

Let us leave these schools of thought that use affirmations and denials. The best affirmation and the only effective one is an assumption which, in itself, implies denial of the former state.

The best denial is total indifference. Things wither and die through indifference. They are kept alive through attention.

You do not deny a thing by saying it does not exist. Rather you put feeling into it by recognizing it. And what you recognize as true, is true to you – be it good, bad or indifferent.

35

Is it possible for one to appear dead and still not be dead?

General Lee was supposed to have been born two years after his mother, believed to be dead, was buried alive. Lucky for her she was not embalmed or buried in the earth, but in a vault where someone heard her cry and released her. Two years later Mrs. Lee bore a son who became General Lee. That is part of this country's history.

36

How could one who was deprived in his youth become a success in life?

We are creatures of habit, forming patterns of the mind which repeat themselves over and over again. Although habit acts like a compelling law which drives one to repeat the patterns, it is not a law, for you and I can change the patterns.

Many successful men such as Henry Ford, Rockefeller and Carnegie were deprived in their youth. Many of the great names in this country came from poor families, yet they left behind them great accomplishments in the political, artistic and financial world.

One evening a friend of mine attended a meeting for young advertising executives. The speaker of the evening said to these young men, "I have but one thing to say to you tonight, and that is to make yourself big and you cannot fail."

Taking an ordinary fish bowl, he filled it with two bags, one of English walnuts and the other of small beans. Mixing them with his hand, he began to shake the bowl and said, "This bowl is life. You cannot stop its shaking, as life is a constant pulsing, living rhythm – but watch."

And as they watched the big walnuts came to the top of the bowl as the little beans fell to the bottom.

Looking into the bowl the man asked, "Which one of you is complaining, asking why?" Then added, "Isn't it strange, the sound is coming from the bowl and not the outside. A bean is complaining that if he had had the same environment as the walnut he, too, would do big things, but he never had the chance."

Then he took a little bean from the bottom of the bowl and placed him on top saying, "I can move the bean through sheer force, but I cannot stop the bowl of life from shaking."

And as he shook the bowl, the little bean once again slid to the bottom.

Hearing another voice of complaint he asked, "What's that I hear? You are saying that I should take one of those big fellows who thinks he is so big and put him on the bottom and see what happens to him? You believe he will be just as limited as you because he will be robbed of the opportunity of big things just as you are? Let's see."

Then the speaker took one of the big walnuts and pushed him right down to the bottom of the bowl, saying, "I still can't stop the bowl from shaking."

And as the men watched the big walnut came to the top again.

Then the speaker added, "Gentlemen, if you really want to be successful in life, make yourself big."

My friend took this message to heart and began to assume he was a successful businessman. Today he is truly a big man if you judge success by dollars. He now employs over a thousand people in the city of New York. Each one of you can do what he did. Assume you are what you want to be. Walk in that assumption and it will harden into fact.

Part of the
NEVILLE EXPLAINS THE BIBLE
Series

Other books in the series include:

Freedom For All
Prayer: Believe to Receive
Meditation: The Joyful Art of Persistence

Taught by Neville Goddard
Edited by Tim Grimes

Made in United States
North Haven, CT
18 April 2022

18360599R00065